Becoming a Disciple

First Principles of the Faith

by Jeff Reed

A six-session Bible study for small groups

THE FIRST PRINCIPLES

LearnCorp Resources is committed to assisting churches, parents, Christian schools,
and Christian businessmen and women with resources to carry out their ministries.

These materials are designed to integrate with BILD-International resources, which
are designed to help churches train leaders.

Art direction and design: Bill Thielker

Background cover image: used by permission of Word Publishing, Dallas TX.

All Scripture, unless otherwise noted, is from the New American Standard Bible.

Edition 1.2

ISBN 1-891441-00-0

Table of Contents

PREFACE – A Living Story

This series has grown out of the labor of many faithful believers. It has been developed in the context of the ministry of establishing churches for over 25 years. The story of its development is truly a living story, filled with faithful men and women serving Jesus Christ as they build their lives, families, and churches upon these first principles.

A first word of thanks goes to my immediate family. To my wife, Nancy, who has taught me the true meaning of faithfulness. To the editing team, which is made up of the three generations of women in my life—Nancy, my mother-in-law Maxine, and my daughter Anna—whose lives truly adorn the gospel. Without this team, the booklets would not be grammatically correct or readable. In addition, thanks to my son Jonathan, who is diligently laboring to make this series live for high school students, and to my son-in-law George Stagg, who has overseen the entire publishing project. Both are emerging as faithful, young ministers of the gospel.

A word of thanks to my church family—Ontario Bible Church—who have endured the endless development of this material over the 25 years, beginning with ugly green notebooks. This small, faithful group of believers have built their lives on the first principles of the faith and are now reaping the fruit of their labor in the lives of their children and in a worldwide ministry.

A word of thanks to all the leaders and churches who are part of BILD International's worldwide network, who have faithfully used and contributed to the development of BILD resources from which this series is developed and in which it is designed to be integrated. Already several translation projects have begun to place this series in other languages. Special thanks to Don McReavy, who goaded me into producing the initial Establishing Series, and who continues to labor with me in its development.

A word of thanks to my two partners in LearnCorp Resources—Bob Goris and Charlie Stagg. Just as many strategic people helped make the apostle Paul's journeys possible, they have invested significant resources to make this series a reality. In addition, thanks to Bill Thielker, an outstanding designer who truly seeks to be faithful to the skills and craft that God has entrusted to him.

On behalf of the entire church family listed above, it is our prayer that God will use this series as a modern day didache—or catechism if you will—to help establish tens of thousands, if not hundreds of thousands, in the first principles of the faith, that their churches might multiply and their families produce fruit for generations to come.

Jeff Reed
October, 1997

BECOMING A DISCIPLE –
Introduction

The concept of becoming a disciple is central to the entire message and mission of Jesus Christ. The term disciple is a very colorful word, painting a clear picture of what it means to become a follower of Jesus Christ. After having been crucified and resurrected from the dead, Jesus gave His followers—the disciples—a clear command: to go to the whole world and make disciples. One of the clearest accounts of this command is recorded in Matthew 28:19,20:

> 19) Go therefore and make disciples of all the nations, baptizing them in the name of the Father and the Son and the Holy Spirit, 20) teaching them to observe all that I commanded you; and lo, I am with you always, even to the end of the age.

In this command, Jesus laid out His mission for the church. The specific command was to make disciples. What exactly does the term disciple mean? There are two main ideas in the term disciple:

- A follower, an adherent
- A pupil, apprentice

The first aspect of disciple is that of becoming a follower, an adherent—becoming a follower of a person and an adherent of his teaching. Secondly, it pictures one who is a pupil, an apprentice. It therefore describes one who is learning the teaching. Both of these ideas seem to be part of Jesus' command.

In this command, Jesus also explains how to make disciples. He tells them to go, baptize, and teach. They are to go—to take the message of Jesus Christ to all nations. They are to baptize—to publicly identify the believers with Jesus, His teaching, and His community of followers. They are to teach—to carefully apprentice them in the teachings of Jesus Christ.

This booklet is designed to take you through a simple process of examining the Bible for yourself and carefully thinking through what it means to become a disciple of Jesus Christ. It is also designed to bring you to a point of commitment, of fully embracing the faith—the teachings of Jesus Christ.

In session one, we will study the gospel—the basic message that one must believe in order to receive forgiveness of sins and become part of the family of God. Fully accepting the gospel is the first step toward becoming a disciple. We will examine the second step—baptism—in session two. In the third session, we will look at the essentials of the teaching. The early followers of Christ referred to this teaching as *the didache* (Greek for "the teaching"). The Apostles delivered this teaching, and each believer was to be apprenticed in it. We will consider the importance of internalizing the teaching, in the fourth session. The teaching was not just content to be learned, but was intended to shape and transform the disciples' lives. In the fifth session, the subject will be lifestyle issues—how to live and relate in the world.

In one sense, becoming a disciple means to become a follower of Jesus Christ, which starts with initial belief in the gospel. In a fuller sense, becoming a disciple means to become a pupil, an apprentice of Jesus Christ and His teaching. An apprentice must master the teaching of the master. So let's begin the process of becoming true disciples.

THE FIRST PRINCIPLES SERIES

The Demands of Today's Fast-Paced Society

We are entering a whole new way of life—computers, endless streams of information, new work realities—which demands continuous learning. This environment puts tremendous pressure on our time, finances, and relationships.

As Christians, we are under even more pressure. Besides making a living in this society and doing a good job in our homes and marriages, there is the extra desire to serve God, which includes having an effective ministry. Students have to juggle assignments, work hours, and family involvement, as well as involvement in a local church and the tremendous opportunity for ministry amongst peers. This involves more time and resources—in our homes, in the workplace, at school, and directly in the lives of our local church communities. There seems to be little time for our own personal growth and development.

Our culture builds into us a mindset about so many things, one of which is our personal development.

We want quick fixes—not long term solutions.
We want how to's—not the ability to think clearly.
We want short training—not lifelong learning.
We want tantalizing subjects—not serious ordered learning.
We want fill-in-the-blank exercises—not reflective writing.
We want one-time applications—not serious projects.

If we are going to be effective as Christians in the coming century, we must carve out regular time for personal growth and development. This cannot be neglected if we expect significant fruit to come from our lives. We must have some sort of strategy that will help guide us lifelong. And we must take the first step.

The First Principles Series is designed to be just such a first step. Now on to the first step!

Design of The First Principles Series I-III

This booklet is part of a set of four booklets, which make up Series I. The whole collection, Series I-III, totals thirteen booklets. They are all built around an idea found in Paul's letter to the church at Colossae written almost 2000 years ago.

> See to it that no one takes you captive through philosophy and empty deception, according to the tradition of men, according to the elementary principles of the world, rather than according to Christ. (Colossians 2:8)

The phrase "the elementary principles" is best translated "the first principles." They are the basic fundamentals of the faith. They represent the first things that must be learned, upon which everything else is built. If they are not carefully understood, everything else will be distorted. The writer of the letter to the Hebrews understood this when he exhorted the Hebrew Christians who were forgetting their newfound faith, in Hebrews 5:

> 11) Concerning him we have much to say, and it is hard to explain, since you have become dull of hearing. 12) For though by this time you ought to be teachers, you have need again for someone to teach you the elementary principles of the oracles of God, and you have come to need milk and not solid food. 13) For everyone who partakes only of milk is not accustomed to the word of righteousness, for he is a babe. 14) But solid food is for the mature, who because of practice have their senses trained to discern good and evil.

The Hebrew Christians forgot *the first principles* of their faith. Once they became Christians, their Jewish family members and friends put tremendous pressure on them to return to Judaism and began challenging the basics of the Christian faith. It is clear from this passage that it is impossible to move on toward maturity without carefully understanding the first principles.

This series of booklets is designed to lead you through the first principles so that you can build upon them and grow on toward maturity. In every generation of churches since the time of the New Testament, believers were expected to learn these first principles. In the early church, before new believers were accepted into the church, they needed to learn *the didache* ("the teaching"). "The Didache" was a summary of the basic teaching of the New Testament—the first principles. During the Reformation (1500's), this teaching was called catechism, again designed to help Christians master the first principles.

Actually, the concept of first principles is important in every area of life. It is central to all quality education. Almost 150 years ago, in the classic work *The Idea of the University*, John Newman referred to a concept he called "pushing up the first principles." According to Newman, the purpose of a university is to teach the first principles of every discipline and then to explore the full limits of those first principles—pushing the principles up through all levels of research.

So it is with our Christian faith. Once we have mastered the first principles, we are able to push them up through all areas of our lives. That is, we are ready to move on to maturity. *The First Principles Series* is carefully designed to help you lay the foundation of your faith.

Whether you are a new believer, a believer who needs to have these first principles laid carefully for the first time, or for whatever reason, need to have them laid afresh, do your work carefully and you will reap a lifetime of benefits.

The First Principles

Series I

1. Becoming a Disciple
   First Principles of the Faith

2. Belonging to a Family of Families
   First Principles of Community Life

3. Participating in the Mission of the Church
   First Principles of Community Purpose

4. Cultivating Habits of the Heart
   First Principles of Disciplined Living

Series II

1. Enjoying Your Relationship
   First Principles of Marriage

2. Passing on Your Beliefs
   First Principles of Family Life

3. Envisioning Fruitful LifeWork
   First Principles of Ministry

4. Building for Future Generations
   First Principles of True Success

Series III

1. Handling the Word with Confidence
   First Principles of Bible Study

2. Unfolding the Great Commission
   First Principles from Acts

3. Laying Solid Foundations in the Gospel
   First Principles from 1 & 2 Thessalonians

4. Catching God's Vision for the Church
   First Principles from Ephesians

5. Living in God's Household
   First Principles from the Pastorals

Design of the Study Guides

This series is designed to lead you through a learning process—a process designed to teach you to think. This process is based upon the Hebrew wisdom model in the Bible (the Bible's educational literature) and on sound, contemporary, educational research. It is used in all of LearnCorp's Bible studies, so once you have mastered the process it will serve you for all of your future work in these and subsequent series. It will also provide a natural study model that you can apply to all areas of your life.

The first five weeks, you will follow a four-step study process. The sixth week is a summary session and final step. You will "pull together" all of your work from the first five weeks into a final project and share it in your small group.

Consistent Study Process (CSP)

A Consistent Study Process (CSP) is used in these books to take you through a complete learning cycle every time you study a passage or concept in the Scriptures. CSP can also serve as a convenient reminder that Bible study is not ESP—we are not trying to mystically experience the text, but to carefully and soundly study the text. There are four basic steps to this process and one final step that integrates the work from the first four.

The First Five Weeks: In the first five sessions of every First Principles study guide, the four basic steps will be done each week: 1) Study the Scriptures, 2) Consult the Scholars, 3) Think Through the Issues, and 4) Apply the Principles.

The importance of each step is explained below.

Study the Scriptures

This step is foundational. We cannot begin exploring the issues of the Bible without first understanding exactly what the passages mean. Discussion groups in which everyone simply shares his opinion are disrespectful of the Scriptures, and therefore to God. They are often merely a pooling of ignorance.

You will go through this same first step in every session, in every booklet. You will begin with a passage to read, answer a few basic questions about the passage, and finally summarize the core teaching of the passage.

Your work in this step:
- Read the passage.
- Think through the questions.
- Summarize the core teaching of the passage.

Consult the Scholars

This step is very important as well, although it is not always highly valued by Christians in our generation. God raises up teachers and scholars to serve in every generation. These teachers can do great harm or great good to churches. We have provided you with some solid, carefully chosen research—in nugget form—to stimulate your thinking. These nuggets of research take two forms. One is a brief commentary on the passage. The other consists of several short instructional quotes on the ideas related to the core truths of the passage.

Your work in this step:
- Read and reflect on the brief commentary.
- Read and reflect on the key quotes.
- Record any insights from the readings.

Think Through the Issues

This step is designed to help you think through the implications of the core teaching of the passage that you have been studying. Unless we go through this process, we can gloss over the significance of the core truths—the first principles of the faith. This is best done in a small group where issues can be discussed thoroughly. Debate an issue in light of the biblical text and try to come to one conclusion as a group. It is not a time for airing opinions but for genuine interaction with the issues.

Your work in this step:
- Think through the issue before discussion.
- Record initial thoughts on the issue before discussion.
- Discuss the issue in your small group.
- Record final thoughts after the discussion.

Apply the Principles

This step brings the basic learning cycle to completion. It is not enough to gain a clear grasp of an issue. It is not enough to accurately understand the core truths of a passage or verse in the Bible. We must apply it to our lives. Applications should be specific and related to the core truths of the passages studied.

Your work in this step:
- Think back through the first three steps.
- Design an application for your life.

The Sixth Week: The last session in each study guide is the final step.

Reshaping Our Lives

This step brings together the entire study process. In each of the first five weeks, we moved through the 4-step Consistent Study Process (CSP). Now in the sixth week, you will pull together all of your work and evaluate your whole life.

Too often today, we stop short of what is necessary to really change our lives. Thinking through simple applications is very important as we study the Bible, but thinking through our whole lives in light of these new truths is essential. The final step in the study process requires that we rethink our entire lives in light of the truths we have been studying— that we rearrange our worldview. We must allow the truths to reshape every aspect of our lives.

Your work in this step:
- Commit your heart—by reflection, personal journaling, and prayer.
- Commit your mind—by forming clear convictions and memorizing Scripture.
- Commit your life—by decisions, personal projects, and life habits.

Two Final Parts of the Study Guides: Each study booklet contains two additional parts—a glossary and a lifelong learning section.

Glossary of Key Biblical Terms and Concepts—The glossary is designed to help you with important terms that you may have encountered for the first time in your study. They are kept to a minimum in the guides, but it is not possible or preferable to remove all terms with special meaning. New terms—especially biblical terms full of rich truths—just have to be learned. To make this process easier, we have included a glossary.

Lifelong Learning—This final section introduces you to additional resources that you may want to pursue. After completing a study guide, it is crucial that you do not view yourself as finished. You must understand that you are laying foundations for a lifetime of learning. Several resources are recommended for your further development.

THE GOSPEL MESSAGE
SESSION 1

Embracing the gospel is the first step in becoming a disciple. The gospel literally means "good news"—the good news of Jesus Christ. Before we can proceed in our Christian faith, we must understand the gospel in its simplest form—the way the apostles taught it to the early church. We will begin this study booklet, *Becoming a Disciple*, by studying a passage in Acts 10:34-48. This is one of Peter's sermons; in fact, it is the very first gospel presentation to the Gentiles (all non-Jewish people). This message by Peter is an excellent example of the gospel that was proclaimed by the apostles. The early church referred to the gospel proclaimed as the *kerygma* (the New Testament Greek word for "proclamation"). Before anyone was baptized and received into the churches, they needed to understand the kerygma.

 Study the Scriptures

Read the Passage: Acts 10:34-48

Think Through the Questions:

1. What was the core content of the message that Peter preached? What exactly did he say about Jesus?

2. What did Peter say they needed to do to have their sins forgiven? Believe what?　Believe in Jesus

3. What happened to them when they believed?
Received the Holy Spirit

Summarize the Core Teaching of the Passage:

Write a paragraph, outline, annotate, or chart your conclusions—whatever best communicates for you. Be sure to comment on the content of Peter's message, especially concerning who Christ was and what was required for forgiveness of sins.

Core teaching of Acts 10:34-48:

1. God shows no favoritism

2. He accepts those who fear Him & do right

3. There is peace w/ God through Christ

4. God anointed Jesus w/ Holy Spirit + power

5. Apostles were witnesses of all Jesus did

6. Jesus died on a cross, but God raised Him

7. Jesus appeared to the apostles

8. Jesus instructed them to testify as to who Jesus was - Judge of all

9. Those who believe in Jesus have their sins forgiven

10. Holy Spirit fell on those Gentiles who believed

11. They spoke in tongues   12. They were baptized

Consult the Scholars

The following comments are designed to help you better understand the passage and to stimulate your thinking on the implications of the teaching.

Read and Reflect on this Brief Commentary on Acts 10:34-48:

It is important to understand the context of Peter's message in Acts. You may want to take time to read the context—Acts 10:1-11:18. Up to this time in Acts, the gospel had only gone out to the Jewish people in Jerusalem and eventually to the surrounding areas. About 40,000 had become Christians in Jerusalem, but there were still no Gentile believers. This whole narrative about Cornelius, which began in Acts 10:1, is about the gospel going to the Gentiles for the first time.

Cornelius was a Roman (Gentile) military man who was a religious type. He looked favorably on the Jewish people, even giving money to them. He genuinely sought to know God. However, Peter was slow to take the gospel to the Gentiles, as were most of the other church leaders. Therefore, God stepped in through a dream, directing Peter to go to Cornelius' house. When he got there, Cornelius asked to hear the gospel.

So what did Peter tell him? The essential facts Cornelius needed to know about Jesus Christ:

- Jesus was sent to Israel by God.
- He went about doing good.
- The Jews put Him to death—but God raised Him up.
- The apostles saw Him, ate with Him, and He ordered them to preach this message.
- He is the judge of the living and the dead—and all who believe (trust) in Him will have their sins forgiven.
- All of this was predicted by the prophets in the Old Testament (over 300 prophecies predicted the person and work of Jesus Christ in the Old Testament).

Every message in Acts given by Peter and Paul focused on the person and work of Jesus Christ. This is what the early church called the *kerygma*—the proclamation. All who believed in the proclamation were considered true believers.

The Gentiles in Cornelius' house believed (inferred here, stated in Acts 11:17), received the Spirit of God, and finally were baptized. The Spirit was given to those who believed and came to live in them, as Jesus had promised in John 13-17. In this instance, the mark of receiving the Spirit was speaking in tongues. God gave this same sign to the Jewish believers when they received the Spirit in Acts 2. In this instance, this phenomenon—speaking to someone in his own language, a language that the speaker did not know—was a sign to the Jewish people of God, and was predicted in the Old Testament. This sign is what helped convince them that the gospel was really going to the Gentiles (Acts 11:13-18).

What is clear from the passage? The message is clear—Jesus is the judge of all of life, and He will forgive the sins of all who believe in Him. Once we believe, we receive the Spirit of God. Then we need to be baptized, which is a sign of identifying with Christ and His new believing community—the Church. In sessions 2 and 3 we will deal with the issue of baptism and the work of the Spirit in our lives.

Read and Reflect on Key Quotes:

"...C. H. Dodd, one of the greatest New Testament scholars this century, has shown that there was a basic pattern underlying the early preaching of the gospel. It was a rough outline, which of course was not slavishly followed, but provided a basic structure for the preachers to memorize and use as they thought fit. This pattern they used ran something like this (consult Dodd's book *The Apostolic Preaching and Its Developments* for the details). 'The age of fulfillment has dawned, as the Scriptures foretold. God has sent His messiah, Jesus. He died in shame upon a cross. God raised him again from the tomb. He is now Lord, at God's right hand. The proof of this is the Holy Spirit whose effects you see. This Jesus will come again at the end of history. Repent, believe, and be baptized.'"[1]

This is taken from Michael Green's book *Evangelism Now & Then*. Green is an Englishman who has developed an expertise in evangelism and the early church.

In *The Apostolic Preaching and Its Developments*, by C. H. Dodd, there is a summary of the Kerygma of Paul. Dodd compiled Paul's teaching and wrote it in credal form:

"The prophecies are fulfilled, and the new Age is inaugurated by the coming of Christ.

He was born of the seed of David.

He died according to the Scriptures, to deliver us out of the present evil age.

He was buried.

He rose on the third day according to the Scriptures.

He is exalted at the right hand of God, as Son of God and Lord of quick and dead.

He will come again as Judge and Savior of men."[2]

This is basically what is recorded in the sermons in Acts and in the gospel summaries in Paul's letters to the churches. This is the essence of the gospel proclaimed by the apostles. If the early converts really believed this, you can see why it changed their whole view of life.

Record any insights from the brief commentary and quotes:

I am reminded that the message of the gospel is simple. Often we complicate it when we share it.

Kerygma - preaching
proclaim - announce
(ke-RIG-ma)

Think Through the Issues

Too often today, the gospel is presented in a way that is significantly different from how it was presented in the New Testament. In our culture, we market everything—even the gospel. To get people to buy it, we want to explain it in simple steps, often without the entire picture. The questions below will guide you in thinking through and discussing what it means to embrace the gospel in today's world.

Issue: Your own reception of the gospel

Think Through the Issue Before Discussion:

1. How was the gospel first explained to you? Was it different from what you have studied so far in this guide? *It was explained this way.*

2. Did those who shared the gospel with you leave any parts out? Which ones? *No.*

3. Why do you think the apostles included all of the elements they did in their gospel proclamation? *All is important. They wanted others to see that Gentiles were included.*

4. When encountering the gospel, what might be possible effects of not getting the whole picture? *Misunderstanding your position w/ God. Might seem more complicated - works stuff*

Record your initial thoughts on the issue before discussion:

I'm glad that I was led to Christ in such a straightforward — by the Bible-way. It was clear and not complicated by other things.

Discuss the issue in your small group.

Record your final thoughts on the issue after discussion:

Apply the Principles

    It is now time to respond to what you have studied and discussed. Take your time on this section.

Think Back Through the First Three Steps.

Design an Application for Your Life.

Complete the assigned project and record any additional applications.

There are two aspects to the assigned project. The first part is to write your summary of the gospel message. The second part is to record your testimony and a commitment to share it with someone.

Jesus was sent by God. He was crucified but God raised him up. He is the Lord of all and all who believe in Him have forgiveness of sins and eternal life.

It is possible, at this point, that you may not be ready to receive the gospel. If that is the case, here are several recommendations for your continued search.

1. Read the Gospel of John

2. Read one of the following books:

      a. *Mere Christianity*, by C. S. Lewis

      b. *Loving God*, by Charles Colson

Wanda - having procedure - asked for prayer

BAPTISM—THE NEXT STEP
SESSION 2

Baptism is the next step in becoming a disciple. Why baptism? Wasn't that just a thing they did in their culture way back then? Baptism is neglected in many churches today. We live in an individualistic culture in which a sense of community is often lost. Identification with a group—although very much needed in our lives—is often placed a distant second to our individual concerns, needs, and aspirations. But what does baptism have to do with the gospel? Moreover, what does it have to do with the concept of community? In our first passage, Acts 10:34-48, we saw that the new believers were ordered to be baptized immediately. In this session we will study Matthew 28:16-20. This is one of the passages commonly called "The Great Commission," since Jesus commanded the disciples to go out and make more disciples. He told them essentially how to do it, and one part of His instruction included baptism. Let's examine the issue and attempt to understand what is so important about this concept.

 ## Study the Scriptures

Read the Passage: Matthew 28:16-20

Think Through the Questions:

1. How were they to make disciples? What were the steps that they were to follow? *Go, Baptizing them, teaching them*

2. Who were they to make disciples from? How far was the message of Jesus to spread? *all the nations*

3. Why was baptism so important? *Jesus commanded it.*

Summarize the Core Teaching of the Passage:
Write a paragraph, outline, annotate, or chart your conclusions—whatever best communicates for you. Be sure to comment on the steps needed to make disciples and why baptism is a part.

Core teaching of Matthew 28: 16-20:

Jesus instructed the disciples to go and make disciples of all the nations. They were told to baptize them and teach them to obey all the things Jesus had commanded. Baptism acknowledged their decision to be a follower of Jesus.

Consult the Scholars

The following comments are designed to help you better understand the passage and to stimulate your thinking on the implications of the teaching.

Read and Reflect on this Brief Commentary on Matthew 28:16-20:

As mentioned above, this is the classic passage that is commonly called "The Great Commission." This commission appears in the gospels of Matthew, Mark, and Luke. Matthew is the most quoted.

The grammatical structure of this commission is very important. The specific command is to "make disciples." The other three parts that support the command are participles—going, baptizing, and teaching. Therefore, there were three things that the disciples needed to do to make disciples of Jesus Christ. First, they were to go to the nations. They had to take the gospel message to them. Second, they needed to baptize those who believed. And third, they needed to teach the new converts all that Jesus had taught them.

Baptism then, is the second of three steps. What exactly is baptism? The word in Greek (the New Testament was originally written in Greek) literally means "to immerse, to dip." Baptism was a practice of immersing an individual in water. It was symbolic. It symbolized becoming a follower of a teacher or the teaching he was proclaiming. Second, it symbolized identifying with a new way of life, a new people. For example, when a Gentile converted to Judaism, he was baptized.

The practice of becoming a disciple of Jesus, as commanded by Jesus, included believing, being baptized, and then being taught. This was the practice of the early churches. The Ethiopian eunuch (Acts 8:34-40), the household of Cornelius (Acts 10:44-48), and the household of the Philippian jailer (Acts 16:31-34) are key examples. The practice symbolized two things. First, the one getting baptized was publicly identifying with Jesus Christ and His message. He believed it! Being immersed in water and brought back up out of the water pictured the death, burial, and resurrection of Christ. He was being resurrected to a new life. Second, He was identifying with the new community. When he came back up out of the water and embraced those waiting for him, he was part of a new family, a new community of believers.

Baptism was essential because it reinforced the decision to trust in the person and work of Jesus Christ and to publicly identify with His new community of believers—the Church. The new convert was then received into a local church community. (The local church community is dealt with in the next booklet in this series—*Belonging to a Family of Families.*)

23

To become a disciple of Jesus Christ means first to believe in the person and work of Jesus Christ—the gospel; to be publicly baptized—identifying with Jesus and His message and joining the community of faith; and finally, to receive the teachings which Jesus taught the disciples.

Read and Reflect on Key Quotes:

"First, believers were baptized into the church. We read that on the birthday of the church 'those who received (Peter's) word were baptized, and there were added that day three thousand souls' (Acts 2:41). Unless Luke was being very impressionistic, it is clear that someone actually counted these new Christians. Their faces were recognized, their names assimilated. Somebody took an interest in them, and they were baptized into the church. Repentance and faith were not enough. They needed to undergo the rite of initiation that Jesus Himself had inaugurated. They were baptized. That is the badge of Christian belonging, and it should be conferred as soon as possible after the person is clearly committed to Christ. At least, that is what the early Christians believed. They baptized upon profession of faith...

"Before we leave the controversial subject of baptism (on which I have tried to write more comprehensively in my book *Baptism*), it ought to be noted that baptism is never an isolated act separated from the life of the church of God. It is the doorway into that church, and this is very evident in a Jewish or Muslim community when people are baptized. They can believe in Jesus until the cows come home, and nobody gets upset. It is when they cross the Rubicon of baptism that the insults begin to fly, and usually the candidates are thrown out of house and home, disinherited, and a funeral is held for them. Baptism is inescapably corporate. It brings you into the Christ in whom others are engrafted. So it should not be administered without the intention of incorporation into the church of God. That is what happened at Pentecost. Those who responded to Peter's sermon were baptized and added to the church."[3]

This quote was taken from "Christian Nurture," chapter 11 in *Evangelism Through the Local Church*, by Michael Green.

"Baptism is and always was the church's initiation-rite ('Initiation,' from a Latin word for 'beginning,' means reception and entrance into committed membership.) Yes; but what exactly is baptism? And why does it matter?

"Baptism is a set action with water and words. By pouring, sprinkling, or immersing, the candidate is momentarily put beneath water, and then brought 'out from under.' The Greek word baptizo means literally 'dip,' and the action suggests both washing and a new start. The accompanying words—'in the name of the Father, and of the Son, and of the Holy Spirit'—announce a relationship in which the candidate is both claimed by and committed to the Triune God.

"Pagan religions have washing rituals, and think them important for changing people's inward state. But Christianity says that the inward change which counts before God is a matter of faith—not just correct belief, either, but a living heart-commitment to God through Jesus Christ. This change is not produced by any particular ritual, for it does not depend on any ritual at all. Rituals in emergency are dispensable anyway, and no ritual can help us while we deny or defy God in our hearts. The apostles baptized believers and their dependents, but insisted that what saves is faith—'Believe in the Lord Jesus, and you will be saved' (Acts 16:14ff.; cf. verses 29-33).

"But if you can believe and be saved without baptism, why does the church require baptism?...

"For baptism is among Jesus' commands. He sent His followers to disciple all nations, baptizing them in the triune name (Matthew 28:19). So a church that did not require baptism, and an unbaptized Christian who did not ask for it would be something of a contradiction in terms. The root reason for the practice of baptizing is to please Jesus Christ our Lord."[4]

This quote is from "Entering In: Baptism and Conversion," a section in *Growing in Christ*, by J. I. Packer. Packer is best known for his classic work, *Knowing God*, which ought to be read by every Christian several times throughout his or her lifetime.

Record any insights from the brief commentary and quotes:

Baptized and added to the church

Baptism was commanded by Jesus -
We do it to be obedient

Think Through the Issues

Today, when an individual becomes a Christian, baptism is often ignored. This may be true partially because we are an individualistic society and often know very little about true community. Our salvation is a personal matter. Most discipleship material bypasses or only gives a token nod to baptism and the need for the local church to be central in our lives as believers. Yet, in the New Testament, baptism was considered very important. The questions below are designed to help you think more deeply about the importance of baptism.

Issue: The meaning and significance of baptism

Think Through the Issue Before Discussion:

1. What part does baptism play in Jesus' command to make disciples? Why?

2. Why do you think baptism is ignored so often in our culture?

3. What might be some of the consequences of ignoring this command? Of obeying it?

Record your initial thoughts on the issue before discussion:

1. Baptism was part of the three part
command - Go - Baptise - Teach

2. It is a more outward sign of our faith
We have to be willing to take a stand
before others
We still want to think we can do it on our
own -

3. Any time we ignore a command we are
missing out on the closeness and
blessing that we could have by obeying

4. When we obey - God blesses us

Discuss the issue in your small group.

Record your final thoughts on the issue after discussion:

Apply the Principles

It is now time to respond to what you have studied and discussed. Take your time on this section.

Think Back Through the First Three Steps.

Design an Application for Your Life.

The obvious application of this session is to decide to be baptized—if you have not already taken that step. Use the space provided to briefly write what you would like to say publicly at your baptism. If you have been baptized, record what you said at your baptism, or what you would have said in light of your study in this session.

Personal Testimony — record what you would say at your baptism in light of your study in this session:

THE FIRST PRINCIPLES
SESSION 3

The final aspect of Jesus' command, to make disciples, is to teach them. Being a disciple is being a follower of Jesus' teaching. The early church called their summary of this teaching "The Didache," or "The Teaching." They believed that there was a core set of teaching of Jesus Christ, which had been delivered by the apostles, which everyone needed to learn. The core elements of this teaching are referred to in the New Testament as "the first principles of Christ." This entire series—thirteen study guides in all—is built upon the concept of "first principles." In this session we are going to study the basic passage where this concept comes from: Colossians 2:6-8. The principles of Christ are set against the principles of this world. If you are going to study these principles throughout 13 study guides, it is essential that you develop a personal conviction that they exist. Note: it would be helpful to review the design of *The First Principles Series* on pages 8-10 at this time.

Study the Scriptures

Read the Passage: Colossians 2:6-8

Think Through the Questions: *healthy, encouraged, stable - secure, stable*

1. What do the images *rooted, built up,* and *established* communicate concerning progressing in our faith? *happiness - core of #1 taking traditions negativity*

holy spirit revealed things

2. What are some of the elementary principles of the world?

3. What are some of the elementary principles of Christ, which you have learned so far? *love others being a servant contentment*

4. What does it mean to be taken captive by a philosophy? *It gets a hold of you - prisoner of it.*

Summarize the Core Teaching of the Passage:

Write a paragraph, outline, annotate, or chart your conclusions—whatever best communicates for you. Be sure to comment on the images used for progressing in our faith. Also, try to define and contrast the principles of the world with the principles of Christ.

Core teaching of Colossians 2:6-8:

Consult the Scholars

The following comments are designed to help you better understand the passage and to stimulate your thinking on the implications of the teaching.

Read and Reflect on this Brief Commentary on Colossians 2:6-8:

This is one of the foundational passages for this whole series. It is important that you understand this passage in its context. This section appears in a letter written by the apostle Paul to one of his young, growing churches—the church at Colossae. This letter is a lot like the letter he wrote to the church at Ephesus. He was concerned that the churches understand fully what had happened to them. He wanted to see them fully understand their calling—their new life in Christ. He wanted them to understand God's overall plan for their lives and fully grasp the importance of the church, that they might not only be stable in their understanding, but also live fruitful lives.

Paul's concern in this passage was the whole sphere of how they lived their lives. The term he used for *walk* literally refers to how one lives his whole life, how he conducts life's affairs. He wanted them to be rooted, built up, and established in their faith. Their "faith in Christ" was not just for their salvation, but it was to permeate every area of their lives. To get this idea across, Paul used the concept of philosophy. The world has a philosophy and Christ has a philosophy. The world's philosophy is built upon the tradition of men—core ideas handed down from generation to generation. For example, we refer to the history of Western thought. Christ has an entire philosophy, which is founded on a different set of principles. Once we buy into a philosophy, it captures us. We then build our whole foundation on that philosophy—whether we are conscious of it or not.

The idea of a philosophy of the world and a philosophy of Christ is made more accessible by the concept of *elementary principles,* as it is translated in the New American Standard Bible. The world has a set of elementary principles, and Christ has a set of elementary principles. The phrase *elementary principles* is literally translated as "first principles" in the Greek. As in any discipline we must master the first principles before moving on to more complicated areas. Once we master the first principles, we have an ability to reason, to explore, to go on to more complicated matters. You might say that we develop "critical judgment" which is principle centered. In Hebrews 5:11-14 (which is the other place where the phrase *elementary principles* is used), the author states that maturity of judgment comes once a person has mastered the first principles. We develop discernment into life's choices. We will be able to live by a set of principles, not a set of rules. This brings tremendous freedom.

Traditions is an interesting word in our passage. It literally means "that which is handed down" by teaching, usually inferring an authoritative or official teaching. It is used by Paul in 2 Thessalonians 2:15: "So then, brethren, stand firm and hold to the traditions which you were taught, whether by word of *mouth* or by letter from us." It refers to the authoritative teaching handed down by the apostles to the churches.

In other letters in the New Testament, it is called "the teaching," "the deposit of sound doctrine," or "the faith."

In the first 100 years after the death of the apostles, the early church referred to this teaching—these first principles—as *the didache* (Greek for "the teaching"). New Christians were expected to learn and master the didache shortly after they became believers.

Essentially, *The First Principles Series* is a modern, 21st century didache. The instructional quote below is a distillation of the first principles found in the apostles' letters to the early churches. Those who master this entire series will in essence be mastering the first principles—the didache—in much the same form as it was delivered to the first churches.

Read and Reflect on Key Quotes:

"We usually think of the Christian message mainly as a set of beliefs, and miss the New Testament's emphasis on the body of teaching about the Christian way of life. Jesus made it a central part of His ministry to instruct His disciples in the life God intended men and women to live (for example, the Sermon on the Mount and the Last Supper discourse). The apostles and the early church leaders made it a central part of their pastoral work to hand on and explain this instruction. Under the inspiration of the Holy Spirit the writers of the New Testament passed on this teaching to the church for all time. It forms the measuring rod for determining the soundness of Christians' lives. As Paul wrote to the Romans, 'Thanks be to God that you who were once slaves of sin have become obedient from the heart to the *standard of teaching* to which you were committed' (6:17; see also 2 Tim. 1:13; 2:2).

"At the core of this daily-life teaching is the understanding that Christ came to make it possible for men and women to become sharers in God's own nature (2 Peter 1:4), to become like Him (Matt. 5:48; 1 John 3:2). The early Christians saw the New Testament teaching about how to live as a continuation and perfection of the teaching given to God's people in the Old Covenant. Jesus' revelation made it possible to live more fully in accord with God's intentions.

"In his book *Gospel and Law*, C. H. Dodd has noted that much of the New Testament follows a pattern: sections giving instruction in the truths of salvation are followed by sections in which the practical consequences are spelled out. The epistles, for example, often begin with teaching about the work of Christ and conclude with directions about how to live as Christians; for instance, Romans, Galatians, Ephesians and 1 Peter. The *kerygma* ('proclamation' of the good news) and further instruction in the realities of the faith can be distinguished from passages presenting the *didache* (practical 'teaching' about living—pronounced did'a kay).

"Dodd identifies seven major propositions in the didache:

1. *The New Testament Christian is enjoined to reform his conduct.* For instance, Paul writes to the Ephesians: 'Put off your old nature, which belongs to your former manner of life and is corrupt through deceitful lusts, and be renewed in the spirit of your minds, and put on the new nature, created after the likeness of God in true righteousness and holiness' (4:22-24; see also Rom. 12:1-2; 13:11-14).

2. *The typical virtues of the new way of life are set forth.* 'But the fruit of the Spirit is love, joy, peace, patience, kindness, goodness, faithfulness, gentleness, self-control' (5:22-23; see also Col. 3:12).

3. *The proper Christian relationships within the family, the primary unit of the Christian community, are reviewed.* 'Wives, be subject to your husbands, as to the Lord.... Husbands, love your wives as Christ loved the church.... Children, obey your parents in the Lord, for this is right' (Eph. 5:22,25; 6:1; see also Col. 3:18-21; 1 Peter 3:1-7).

4. *Right relationships within the Christian community are set forth.* 'Let love be genuine; hate what is evil, hold fast what is good; love one another with brotherly affection; outdo one another in showing honor' (Rom. 12:9-10; see also Col. 3:13-16; Phil. 2:1-4).

5. *A pattern of behavior toward pagan neighbors is described.* 'Conduct yourselves wisely toward outsiders, making the most of the time. Let your speech always be gracious, seasoned with salt, so that you may know how you ought to answer everyone' (Col. 4:5-6; see also 1 Peter 2:12,18).

6. *Correct relationships with constituted authorities are defined.* 'Be subject for the Lord's sake to every human institution, whether it be to the emperor as supreme or to governors as sent by him to punish those who do wrong and to praise those who do right' (1 Peter 2:13-14; see also Rom. 13:1-7).

7. *There is a call to watchfulness and responsibility.* 'Be sober, be watchful. Your adversary the devil prowls around like a roaring lion seeking someone to devour' (1 Peter 5:8; see also Eph. 6:10-18).

"Christ, the apostles, and the leaders of the early church considered the teaching about the Christian way of life to be the norm for Christians. They viewed the *didache* not as a distant ideal but as something that ordinary people would actually live out. Conversion meant new behavior: 'By this it may be seen who are the children of the devil: whoever does not do what is right is not from God, nor he who does not love his brother' (1 John 3:10). 'By their fruits you shall know them' (Matt. 7:20).

"The early church was not perfect. But the early Christians followed the Christian way of life sufficiently well that their distinctiveness—along with their bold announcement of the gospel—brought on them almost three centuries of persecution in the Roman empire, and at the same time helped to attract thousands of men and women to Christ, even though commitment to Him could end in martyrdom.

"In our own day it cannot be said that Christians in the West are following the teaching of Christ in a way that makes them particularly distinct. At a time when Western societies are swinging away from Christian values, Christians' lives are generally failing to become more clearly distinguishable. Rather, as society becomes less Christian, so do Christians' own patterns of life."[5]

This quote is from "A Distinctive Way of Life," by Kevin Perrotta, which is a chapter in *Leading Christians to Maturity*. The book is written by a collection of authors who are very committed to getting back to New Testament Christianity. It is now out of print, but this chapter is available in several BILD resources. See the Lifelong Learning section at the end of this booklet.

Record any insights from the brief commentary and quotes:

Think Through the Issues

In any instructional endeavor, the first principles must be mastered before studying matters that are more complicated. Imagine trying to do advanced algebra without knowing the basic principles of math. However, today we often go through school without mastering the first principles in hardly any of the subjects that we study. Therefore, it is easy to just enter our Christian life thinking that we will pick up a few things here and there. This is not the way that we should approach our new faith. It is important that we get it right. The foundations that we lay will shape the whole future of our lives. The questions below are designed to help you think more deeply about these first principles.

Issue: The importance of first principles

Think Through the Issue Before Discussion:

Piano
ACCTG.

1. When in life have you had to learn a new set of first principles—a new course? A new job? A new sport?

2. If you don't learn the first principles of your faith, what problems might result? *When trial come - make poor decisions avoid false teaching*

3. What kind of commitment do you think it will take to master the first principles of Christianity? How long?

Lifelong - making it a priority.

Record your initial thoughts on the issue before discussion:

Discuss the issue in your small group.

Record your final thoughts on the issue after discussion:

Apply the Principles

It is now time to respond to what you have studied and discussed. Take your time on this section.

Think Back Through the First Three Steps.

Mastering the first principles of the faith—the teaching—cannot be done in just a few days. It takes time—probably a couple of years. Think back through this session and form a conviction about the importance of being founded in the first principles.

Design an Application for Your Life.

In the space provided write your conviction to master the first principles and defend it from Scripture.

Your personal conviction to master the first principles of the teaching and your biblical and logical defense for spending your time in this way:

RENEWING OUR MINDS
SESSION 4

Now that you have made a commitment to master the first principles of the teaching, you need to understand what that means. It is not just information to be learned. Part of becoming a disciple is to "observe" all that He commanded His followers, not just learn it (Matthew 28:19,20). How are the principles to affect our lives? How do we internalize this teaching so that we are truly living by it? These questions will be answered in this unit. God has outfitted us with all that we need to live our lives built upon "The Teaching." He has given us His Word, His Spirit, spiritual gifts, and He created us with natural abilities. All of these work together in a supernatural way to transform our lives, enabling us to walk by the Spirit.

 ## Study the Scriptures

Read the Passage: Romans 12:1-2

dedicated to Him
offered to Him

Think Through The Questions:
1. What does it mean to present our bodies to God as a sacrifice?
2. What does it mean to be conformed to this world? *molded by world* *following its pattern*
3. What is the key to being transformed? What are we to be transformed into? *renewing our mind* *a person following the will of God*

Summarize the Core Teaching of the Passage:

Write a paragraph, outline, annotate, or chart your conclusions— whatever best communicates for you. Comment on what it means to be conformed to this world. From the passage, try to put together a little formula on how to be transformed.

WORD → CHANGES OUR WAY OF
HOLY SPIRIT   THINKING

√

ALLOWS US TO FOLLOW
ALLOWS US TO BECOME MORE
          LIKE JESUS

Consult the Scholars

The following comments are designed to help you better understand the passage and to stimulate your thinking on the implications of the teaching.

Read and Reflect on this Brief Commentary on Romans 12:1-2:

Although this is a brief passage, it is extremely important. It can establish a pattern in your thinking that, if followed faithfully, will enable you to internalize the first principles of Christ's teaching in a life-changing way. In Paul's letter to the church at Rome, this little passage is strategic. In the first eleven chapters of the book of Romans, Paul describes the mercies of God: their salvation (chapters 1-3); their new hope in Christ (chapters 4-5); and their new power to live life in the Holy Spirit (chapters 6-8). Therefore, based upon all of these mercies, 12:1 tells us to "present ourselves to God." The way the passage is written, Paul is calling for a decision. We need to dedicate ourselves to God. The visual picture is that of offering *ourselves* to God instead of some sacrifice.

What exactly does this kind of decision involve? The answer?—an entire transformation of our lives. To get his idea across, Paul sets up a contrast—being conformed to this world versus being transformed. But transformed according to what? Remember the Colossians passage? The world has a set of principles, and Christ has a set of principles (Colossians 2:6-8). They are very different, so you cannot live by both. Earlier in Romans 8:1-16, Paul tells us that we can either set our minds on the things of the Spirit (God's things) or on the things of the flesh (our natural desires tied with this world). This is not a call to give up what we desire and live a boring life by rules and regulations. As we are transformed according to what God wants, we will see for ourselves that God's will is perfect. It will be a far richer life than the world could ever offer.

The concept of being transformed is a very important and very precise one. The literal word is *metamorphidzo* in the Greek, which is where we get the word metamorphosis. It is literally the process of a caterpillar turning into a butterfly. It is written in a way that means that we are allowing someone else to transform us while we do our part—actively renewing our minds. As we renew our minds in the ways of Christ rather than the ways of the world, the Spirit of God gradually transforms us into the image of Christ (cf. 2 Corinthians 3:16-18). How do we renew our minds? We do it by setting our minds on the things of the Spirit in the Word of God, the Bible. If we focus on the principles and philosophies of this world, the world will press us into its mold. If we focus on the principles and philosophies of Christ, the Spirit will transform us into the ways of God, or as Paul says in many of His letters—into the image of Christ. In another passage Paul tells us to be filled with the Spirit (Ephesians 5:18-20), which is done by letting Christ's words saturate our minds (Colossians 3:16-17).

Read and Reflect on Key Quotes:

"Our minds play an exceedingly large role in our Christian lives. It is in our minds that some of our fiercest spiritual warfare takes place. Even the stalwart reformer Martin Luther experienced victories and defeats in his thought life. We are not the first persons to wrestle with spiritual conflicts.

"But the challenge of bringing every thought into the captivity of Christ is an especially difficult one today. Our minds are bombarded by conflicting messages coming to us through diverse media: television, radio, records, films, print, the plastic arts. A collage of impressions and ideas streams through our minds each day, leaving traces in our memories. Sometimes the messages we receive complement and reinforce our Christian convictions. On other occasions, the messages attack our moral standards and sap our spiritual vitality. Sometimes we notice their subtle but devastating effect upon our minds only after months and years have passed.

"Today the need for Christians to renew their minds through prayer, confession, meditation upon God's Word, and participation in the local church is paramount. The apostle Paul put the matter as a command: 'And do not be conformed to this world, but be transformed by the renewing of your mind,' (Romans 12:2)."[6]

John Woodbridge wrote this in the introduction to *Renewing Your Mind in a Secular World*. The book is a series of articles written mostly by professors from Trinity International University in Deerfield, Illinois, one of the best evangelical seminaries in the U.S.

One of the greatest Christian leaders of our day, Francis Schaeffer, has given us the book *True Spirituality* in which he explains the dynamic of Romans 12:1-2:

"There is indeed to be a presenting of our bodies, but this has meaning only on the basis of the understanding of the internal.

"Paul speaks here of not being conformed to this world. But this is not simply externally. In contrast to this, we are to be transformed by the renewing of our mind, and that is internal....

"The work of the Holy Spirit, as the agent of the Trinity, is not a coat we put on. It is not an external thing at all, but internal, bringing in turn something external.

"So here we move on in our understanding of true spirituality in the Christian life. Basically it is a matter of our thoughts. The external is the expression, the result. Moral battles are not won in the external world first. They are always a result flowing naturally from a cause, and the cause is in the internal world of one's thoughts."[7]

Record any insights from the brief commentary and quotes:

Think Through the Issues

We need to internalize and be changed by the first principles of the teaching, but we can not do that on our own. We need the Holy Spirit to be transforming us. The Spirit will supernaturally transform us; however, it is critical that we know our part in the process. What do we need to be doing in order for the Spirit to do His work? The questions below will guide you in thinking through and discussing your responsibility in the transformation process.

Issue: Internalizing the first principles

Think Through the Issue Before Discussion:

HAVING STUFF

1. What are some of the core "principles of the world" that pull on you every day?

2. Since the principles of Christ are supposed to control our new lives, do any of the principles of the world strike you as being contrary to the principles of Christ? Which ones? *CONTENT MEN*

3. What do you need to be doing regularly to truly internalize the principles of Christ so that the Spirit can use them to transform you?

IN WORLD   IN PRAYER   IN FELLOWSHIP

Record your initial thoughts on the issue before discussion:

Discuss the issue in your small group.

Record your final thoughts on the issue after discussion.

Apply the Principles

It is now time to respond to what you have studied and discussed. Take your time on this section.

Think Back Through the First Three Steps.

Design an Application for Your Life.

Mastering the first principles of the teaching of Christ involves more than just learning the concepts. The principles must be internalized. Only the Spirit can transform us; however, we must do our part. The first step is to make a commitment to fully serve God. Record and date your commitment in the space below. Take your time to write it out carefully, because you will review it periodically.

Write your commitment:

LIFESTYLE OF A DISCIPLE
SESSION 5

Jesus upset the entire Jewish establishment by whom He associated with and how He related to the world. He ate and drank with people that the religious people thought He should avoid. He was clearly purpose driven. He wanted everyone to encounter His gospel, and His teaching. And, He wanted His disciples to follow His model. One of the most tragic things that can happen to a new disciple is to be given the impression (by well meaning but greatly misguided believers) that the life of a disciple is basically obeying a set of rules. The rules, expectations, and lifestyles of many churches can become a form of slavery that destroys the spirit of our newfound freedom in Christ. Year by year, these rules build a wall between the nonbelieving world and us. The gospel is supposed to set us free. God intends for us to live by "the first principles" of the faith not "the dirty dozen" for all Christians to avoid. Our faith will be built either upon a rule-based foundation or upon a principle-based foundation. It is crucial for you to understand this so that you will be empowered to stand on your faith and not on the lifestyle opinions of others. The passage in this section—Romans 14:1-23—is the classic passage on living by principles and preserving your freedom in Christ. Master it!

Study the Scriptures

Read the Passage: Romans 14:1-23

fixed or firm belief

Think Through The Questions:

1. What does it mean to have your own convictions before God?

2. What does it mean to judge another? What does it mean to hold another in contempt?   *attitude* — *pass judgement*

3. What does it mean to cause another to stumble?   *form a judgement or opinion of* — *of regarding another as inferior or worthless* — *cause them to sin*

4. What does it mean to be strong in faith? Weak in faith?

Confident trust in   *not as confident*

45

Summarize the Core Teaching of the Passage:

Write a paragraph, outline, annotate, or chart your conclusions—whatever best communicates for you. Comment on the key ideas: personal convictions, judging another and causing another to stumble, and to be strong and weak in faith.

Core teaching of Romans 14:1-23:

Consult the Scholars

The following comments are designed to help you better understand the passage and to stimulate your thinking on the implications of the teaching.

Read and Reflect on this Brief Commentary on Romans 14:1-23:

This passage is part of the section in Romans that began in 12:1-2, which encourages us to be transformed by renewing our minds. Therefore, this teaching is part of renewing our minds. Remember that one of the purposes of renewing our minds is to avoid letting the world press us into its mold. To avoid this, it is important that we learn how to relate to the world around us. We are instructed to dedicate ourselves to God for His service. This means that we must place higher priority on what He thinks than on what others think about how we live and the choices that we make. Notice, in the passage, that we have been given a lot of freedom. And, each of us will give an account for our choices (v. 12). If our faith is strong, then we are able to handle a wider range of choices, all under the idea of serving God fully. Therefore, our choices must be a matter of faith—a matter of personal conviction. If it is not of faith and you go ahead and do whatever you have purposed to do, it is sin (vv. 22-23). That is why it is so important to renew our minds with the Word of God, not men's opinions. We will never be able to make sound lifestyle decisions without at least mastering the first principles.

The argument of this passage seems hard at first, but it is really quite simple. The core ideas are these:

- We each need to develop our own lifestyle convictions—what we eat and drink, whom we associate with, and what special days we observe.
- There is a tremendous amount of lifestyle freedom in Christ.
- We should not judge others by our lifestyle convictions but rather allow them to live before God the way that they feel is proper.
- We should not place those weak in faith in situations where they violate their conscience but allow them to live by their convictions before God.

Keep in mind that Paul is not saying that we can live without any guidelines. After all, we have already established that there is a way of the world and a way of Christ. We need to know the first principles, put them in place, and then make our lifestyle choices. According to this passage, the more mature we are in our understanding of the teaching, the greater freedom we will have in our lifestyles.

Read and Reflect on Key Quotes:

The following quote is taken from "Culture Vultures," chapter 9 in *Gentle Persuasion*, by Joseph Aldrich. This entire book is an excellent introduction to learning to share your faith.

"What do you do when you are faced with some "gray areas"? If you believe your participation in some activity has redemptive potential, and you're sure Scripture doesn't condemn it, what do you do when fellow believers look askance at your proposal? One thing to do is to determine, as best you can, the nature of the objectors. Let me offer a few descriptions that may help.

1. The professional weaker brother/sister.

A legalist by nature, a "professional" weaker brother/sister has taken the easy way out. First, he/she has settled for a simplistic view of spirituality. He believes the mature believer is the one with the smallest comfort zone. Gray doesn't exist for him; his world is black and white. Second, he thinks you demonstrate spirituality by adhering to a narrow, self-imposed list of 'do's' and 'don'ts.' Third, and most serious, all others are expected to conform to this list.

Fourth, this believer is usually a "mature" saint who will not stumble because of the actions of those who reject his petty legalisms. He won't fall into sin because of your deeds; he just doesn't like what you do. Fifth, these folks do more harm than good. They kill joy, resist beauty, and produce ugliness in the name of truth.... They must be confronted in love.

2. The genuine weaker brother/sister.

Folks who are still babes are susceptible to stumbling in the area of doubtful things. We are warned not to put a stumbling block in their path. Children, teenagers, and new believers need careful attention. I think, however, the church as a whole has spent too much time trying to protect our weaker brothers/sisters and not enough time trying to educate them. The weaker brother/sister position is not a lifetime option. It is a developmental period on the way to spiritual maturity.

Susceptible Christians need to understand that they will encounter many within the body of Christ who have lesser or greater amounts of freedom, depending on the issues involved. Once they understand the principle of conscience and the diversity of freedom, they have little excuse to remain a weaker brother/sister. These folks need to be educated. We must not allow them to paralyze our evangelistic efforts.

3. The mature, nonparticipating brother/sister.

These folks limit their liberty for one of two reasons. First, they limit it because they don't have freedom in a particular area. Perhaps they refrain from dancing because they don't have freedom to dance.

That is as it should be. Second, they may limit their liberty despite freedom to exercise it. Wisdom has taught them that it is not necessary, and sometimes is not prudent, to exercise all the liberty, which is theirs to enjoy.... Depending on the issue, we are probably all nonparticipating brothers/sisters.

4. The immature, participating brother/sister.

This person is not necessarily immature in the sense of lacking in knowledge. His immaturity shows up in his injudicious practice and proclamation of freedom. He/she becomes a champion of liberty and attempts to get others to join the larger circle of his/her conscience. These folks harm the cause of Christ by injuring the lambs.

5. The mature, participating brother/sister.

This individual understands the biblical doctrine of liberty and is balanced and mature in its application. He/she is consistent in applying his/her freedom in Christ. Yet, this person is able to exercise freedom in a quiet, nonthreatening manner which attempts to avoid unnecessary offense."[8]

Record any insights from the brief commentary and quotes:

Think Through the Issues

As followers of Christ, it is important to think correctly about how to live and relate in the world around us. We need to have a mature understanding of our freedom in Christ. Yet, there seems to be a lot of confusion about how to live by our personal convictions in light of others who have differing lifestyle convictions. This is an important issue. Give it time in discussion. Make sure that Romans 14 is at the center of your discussion.

Issue: Thinking maturely about your lifestyle as a Christian

Think Through the Issue Before Discussion:

1. What is the difference between a strong and a weak Christian? What is the goal—to be strong or weak?

2. How can we stand on our convictions, live the way we think before God, and not cause another to stumble?

3. If we are mature in our lifestyle choices and understand our freedom in Christ, how might this benefit our witness for Christ?

People see our freedom in Christ rather than us

Record your initial thoughts on the issue before discussion: *adhering to a list of do's + don'ts*

Discuss the issue in your small group.

Record your final thoughts on the issue after discussion:

Apply the Principles

It is now time to respond to what you have studied and discussed. Take your time on this section.

Think Back Through the First Three Steps.

Design an Application for Your Life.

The assigned application is to design your initial "lifestyle philosophy" as a disciple of Jesus Christ. This philosophy will guide you as you begin to serve Christ—the one to whom you have dedicated your life. In light of the argument of Romans 14:1-23, it may be best to write a set of principles. This assumes that you lay a proper foundation of mastering the first principles of the faith.

Write your lifestyle philosophy—as a disciple:

RESHAPING OUR LIVES
SESSION 6

If properly understood, becoming a disciple of Jesus Christ will dramatically reshape our lives. In the first five sessions, we looked at some of the basic elements of becoming a disciple and their significance in our lives. In order to build solidly in our lives as disciples of Jesus Christ, we must embrace the gospel fully. We need to renew our minds with the truth—a full, clear, and accurate understanding of the truth of the gospel. Second, we need to be baptized. And third, we need to think through the core elements of the teaching of Christ—the first principles. We have consistently worked on all of these in the first five sessions.

It is now time to pull together all of our applications from the first five sessions, in order to affect our whole lives. In this fast-paced world, it is hard to find time to do any serious reflection. While we benefited from the exercises in the first five sessions, actually integrating the truths into our lives as a whole takes extra effort. Taken together, they become a powerful force bringing about significant change—change designed to reshape our lives.

 ## Committing Your Heart
Reflection, Personal Journaling, and Prayer

Journaling is an excellent way to reflect more deeply on the significance of what we have been learning. It forces us to express in words what has entered our hearts. It helps us identify and clarify what the Spirit has been using in the Word to enlighten our hearts, as well as to convict us. Prayer should follow this. We should ask God to permanently transform our hearts to give us a desire and longing to grow to maturity.

In this section, think back over your work from each of the five previous sessions. What happened in your life because of your work in each session? Record your thoughts, and reflect on what you wrote. What new convictions have you developed? What have you seen God begin to do in your life? Are there areas that you wish you had followed through on more fully? What affected you most? What convicted you most? What excited you most? How has your philosophy of life changed?

Finally, formulate these thoughts into one main prayer request. If you were to ask God to give you the ability to become a fully committed disciple, how would you ask it? Write the request in a paragraph. Transfer it to a 3 x 5 inch card and carry it with you. Pray over it regularly. Over the next few weeks, record any ways that you see God answering your prayer, on the back of the card.

Your Journal — thoughts on becoming a disciple:

Prayer Request:

Committing Your Mind

Forming Clear Convictions and Memorizing Scripture

It is essential that we pull together what we have studied—formulating our thoughts into clear convictions. What exactly does it mean to become a disciple of Jesus Christ? It is critical that we think clearly about the truths of Scripture. If we have wrong ideas in our heads, then our lives will be built on those wrong foundations. If we misunderstand what it means to be committed disciples, our whole lives may be set on a wrong course. We will probably develop lifestyles that are either conformed to this world, because of the pressure of the world, or separated from this world, because of the pressure of misguided believers who live their lives under a set of do's and don'ts.

Begin by summarizing your studies concerning the process of becoming a disciple into one paragraph—ideally bringing together all of the key truths which you studied in the five sessions. Then, list the essential Bible references to back up your convictions. Finally, choose at least one of these verses to memorize, record it below, and quote it by memory to your study group when you meet. Transfer it to a 3 x 5 inch card—writing the verse(s) and reference on one side and your insights into the verse(s) on the other side. Review it for about 6 weeks.

Becoming a disciple of Jesus Christ—core convictions:

Key verse to memorize:

Committing Your Life
Decisions, Personal Projects, and Life Habits

Think back over the "Apply the Principles" section of each of the five sessions. It is one thing to think about specific applications to our lives as we move through each study. It is another thing to think across our whole lives and begin reshaping our life goals and our lifestyles by what we are learning. This is a vital part of building our lives around the first principles of Christ rather than the first principles of the world.

Several things are necessary in order to integrate these principles into our lives. First, look back over your "Apply the Principles" sections and your work so far in this session. Are there decisions that you need to make? For example, are there life directions that you have been pursuing that you need to change in light of becoming a disciple of Christ? Are there personal projects that come to your mind that would help you more fully embrace the gospel and the teaching? For example, is there a group of friends, or family members that you would like to share the gospel with over the next few months? Are there life habits that you need to build to help you continue to grow as a disciple? For example, do you need a regular time to renew your mind in the Scriptures? If so, write them out in the space below.

Decisions, personal projects, and life habits:

Endnotes

[1] Michael Green, *Evangelism Now and Then* (Downers Grove, IL: InterVarsity Press, 1991) p. 65. Used by permission of the author.

[2] C. H. Dodd, *The Apostolic Preaching and Its Developments* (Kent, England: Hodder & Stoughton Ltd.). Reproduced by permission of Hodder and Stoughton Limited.

[3] Michael Green, *Evangelism Through the Local Church* (Kent, England: Hodder & Stoughton Ltd., 1992) pp. 293-295. Reproduced by permission of Hodder and Stoughton Limited.

[4] J. I. Packer, *Growing in Christ* (Wheaton: Good News/Crossway Books, 1994) pp. 95-97. Used by permission.

[5] Kevin Perrotta, "A Distinctive Way of Life," John Blattner (ed.), *Leading Christians to Maturity*, Ellcott City, MD: Faith & Renewal, 1987, pp. 89-92. Used by permission of the publisher. Renewal Journal and archives are available online at http://www.christlife.org.

[6] John Woodbridge, *Renewing Your Mind in a Secular World* (Moody Bible Institute of Chicago: Moody Press, 1985) pp. ix-x. Used by permission.

[7] Francis A. Shaeffer, *True Spirituality* (Wheaton: Tyndale House Publishers, Inc., 1971) pp. 107, 109-110. All rights reserved.

[8] Joseph C. Aldrich, *Gentle Persuasion* (Portland: Multnomah Publishers, Inc., 1988) Chap. 9, "Culture Vultures," pp. 212-214. Used by permission of Multnomah Press.

Glossary of Key Biblical Terms and Concepts

    The following is a list of important terms that you may have encountered for the first time in this study. Although they are explained in the booklet, it is easy to forget their exact meanings. This glossary can also serve as a catalogue of biblical terms and concepts for future reference.

The Apostles. The twelve disciples, trained by Christ, who, after Christ left the earth, were responsible to take the gospel to the whole world. They were also responsible to lay out the teaching of Christ for all churches and believers in Christ to follow. Acts 2:42.

Baptism. Literally means to immerse someone in water. It symbolizes two truths for the Christian: 1) identifying with Christ and His gospel, and 2) identifying with a Christian community of believers—the church. It is a public practice designed to show others your commitment to Christ and His church. Matthew 28:19-20; Acts 10:44-48.

Christian. "The disciples (the followers of Christ) were first called Christians at Antioch," where the first Gentile church was planted. Therefore, a Christian was synonymous with a disciple. It is true that when one believes the gospel he becomes a child of God, yet to bear the name Christian also infers that one is following Christ and His teachings. Acts 11:26.

Disciple. A follower of Jesus Christ. It refers to one who has received the gospel of Christ, been baptized, and is now following the teaching of Christ. The term initially carries the idea of being an apprentice of the teaching. Matthew 28:19-20.

Didache. (did'-a-kay) Literally means "the teaching" and refers to the teaching delivered by the apostles. This teaching was to be adhered to by all the churches. After the death of the apostles, the early church created a manual called "The Didache" that summarized all the essential teaching of the apostles. Every new believer had to learn this teaching after he was baptized. Acts 2:42.

Established. Used by Paul ("established in your faith") for one who was founded and solidly rooted in the first principles of Christ. It was also used to describe churches that were firmly rooted in the apostles' teaching. Colossians 2:6-8.

First Principles. Translated the "elementary principles" in some translations. It is used as a summary concept that refers to the basic foundational principles that our faith is built upon. The world also has a set of foundational principles that all man's philosophies grow out of. The term comes from two places in the New Testament: Colossians 2:6-8 and Hebrews 5:11-14.

Freedom. A term used for our lifestyle choices. In Christ, we are free to live in and enjoy life in this world. We are to use this freedom to adorn the gospel for nonbelievers who are watching and to use it as a tool to allow us to associate with nonbelievers in a natural way. Romans 14:1-23.

Gospel. Literally means "good news." It refers to the good news about Jesus Christ. That good news is essentially that Christ died on the cross for our sins, was buried and resurrected on the third day, and now everyone who believes in Him has forgiveness of sins. Romans 1:16; 1 Thessalonians 1:5; 2:2,4,8,9.

Great Commission. The phrase used by Christians to summarize Jesus' command to His disciples in Matthew 28:19-20. They were to take the gospel to the whole world, baptizing those who believed, and teaching them the teachings of Christ. This is the mission of the church. Matthew 28:19,20.

Kerygma. (ker-ig-ma) Literally means "the proclamation." It refers to the proclamation of the gospel by the apostles and New Testament church leaders. After the apostles died, the early church used the term to refer to a summary of the exact gospel preached by the apostles, even the form of the message.

Stumble. As taught in Romans 14, it refers to strong believers using their freedom in Christ in such a way that weak believers feel almost pressured to go against their conscience, and thus stumble in their faith. Romans 14:1-23.

The Teaching. The basic teachings of Christ as delivered by the Apostles that all the churches and individual believers in those churches were to study and follow. It is synonymous with "the didache." Acts 2:42.

Transformed. The Greek is "metamorphidzo," which is where we get the word "metamorphosis." It is used in Romans 12:2 for the process that the Spirit of God uses to change us internally, as we renew our minds with the Word—the Bible. Romans 12:1-2.

Weak/Strong. As taught in Romans 14, as Christians, we are either weak or strong. The weak are those who do not fully understand their freedom in Christ and so restrict their lifestyle unnecessarily. The mature operate with a mature understanding of their freedom in Christ and live by principles—living in the world as effective witnesses. Romans 14:1-23.

Lifelong Learning

The booklets of this series are designed to lay the very essential foundations of the faith. They are intended to be just a beginning. The writer of the New Testament letter, Hebrews, reminds us that we are to move on to maturity (Hebrews 5:11-14). This "Lifelong Learning" section is at the end of each First Principles Series booklet. It will serve as a guide to some of the resources that will enable you to build solidly on the foundations laid in each booklet and therefore urge you to press on toward maturity. Review these resources and include any that you would like to read or work through in the "Committing Your Life" section of the sixth session.

1. *Belonging to a Family of Families: First Principles of Community Life,* The First Principles Series I—Book Two

Book two is a follow-up to the booklet you have just completed—Becoming a Disciple. It is very important to follow-up your work in this booklet with book two, so that you understand that becoming a disciple is not an individual effort. Once we become Christians we need to immediately become part of a believing family, a local church—a family of families. In a sense, this booklet builds upon the second session of book one "Baptism—The Next Step." Part of the baptism image is identifying with a community of believers, which is the context for you to grow as a disciple. The early church had no other practice. The local church was at the center of God's mission. This booklet will guide you in becoming a vital part of a family of families.

2. *Becoming Established in the Gospel,* The Establishing Series—Book I

Book I of The Establishing Series is an advanced version of this booklet. The five units of the course parallel the five sessions of this booklet. Many of the articles quoted in the "Key Quotes" of this booklet are included in full in the course, providing a mini-reader. It is an excellent tool for in-depth study in the areas you have begun in this booklet. LearnCorp produces The Establishing Series for BILD International. To order, call BILD International at 1-515-292-7012.

3. *Knowing God,* by J. I. Packer (IVP)

All Christians should read this classic several times in their lives. It describes the gospel in great depth, the work of God the Father, Jesus Christ, and the Holy Spirit so that you can fully understand what the entire Bible teaches on those subjects and how to really know God in a personal way. It is an outstanding example of great teaching and practical application. It is a little difficult to read at points because of some of the terms, so you may want to wait until you have finished the four booklets of this series.

4. *True Spirituality,* by Francis Schaeffer (IVP)

This too is a classic, but very difficult to read at points. Francis Schaeffer was a great Christian thinker (philosopher) who wrote during the 1960's, and addressed issues from a philosophical point of view—addressing the great questions of life from a Christian viewpoint. In this book he deals with the work of the Spirit in our lives, mainly working through the book of Romans. He defines true spirituality as the focus on internal, genuine change, not external conformity.